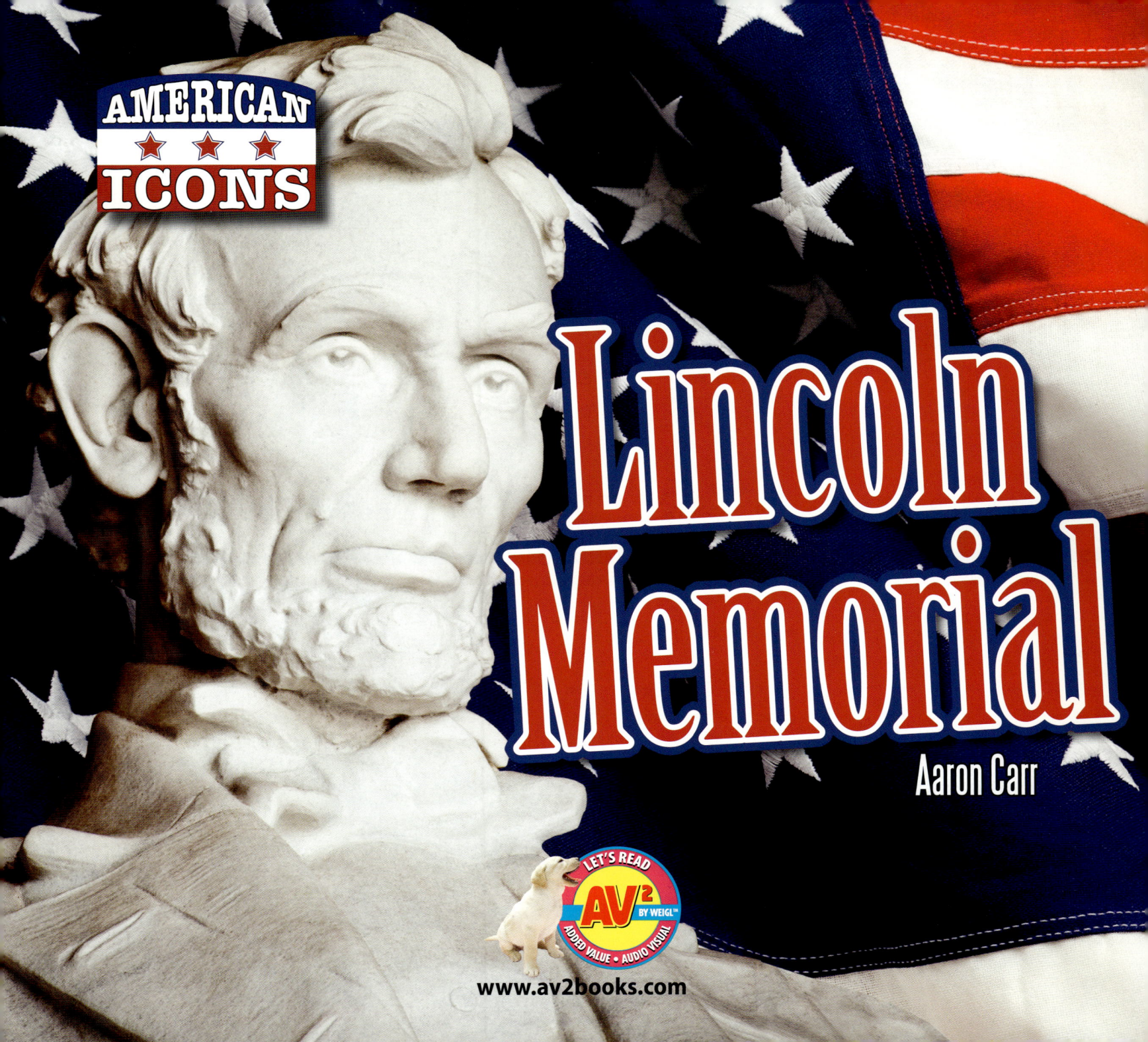

MAI 843 4294

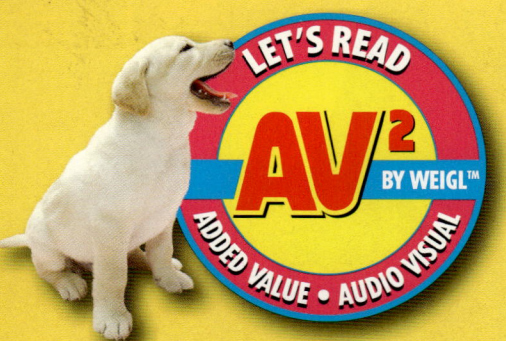

Go to www.av2books.com, and enter this book's unique code.

BOOK CODE

F498351

AV² by Weigl brings you media enhanced books that support active learning.

AV² provides enriched content that supplements and complements this book. Weigl's AV² books strive to create inspired learning and engage young minds in a total learning experience.

Your AV² Media Enhanced books come alive with...

 **Audio**
Listen to sections of the book read aloud.

 **Video**
Watch informative video clips.

 **Embedded Weblinks**
Gain additional information for research.

 **Try This!**
Complete activities and hands-on experiments.

 **Key Words**
Study vocabulary, and complete a matching word activity.

 **Quizzes**
Test your knowledge.

 **Slide Show**
View images and captions, and prepare a presentation.

... and much, much more!

Published by AV² by Weigl
350 5th Avenue, 59th Floor New York, NY 10118
Website: www.av2books.com   www.weigl.com

Copyright ©2014 AV² by Weigl
All rights reserved. No part of this publication may be reproduced, stored in a retrieval system, or transmitted in any form or by any means, electronic, mechanical, photocopying, recording, or otherwise, without the prior written permission of the publisher.

Library of Congress Cataloging-in-Publication Data
Carr, Aaron.
  Lincoln Memorial / Aaron Carr.
     p. cm. -- (American icons)
  ISBN 978-1-62127-202-1 (hardcover : alk. paper) -- ISBN 978-1-62127-206-9 (softcover : alk. paper)
 1. Lincoln Memorial (Washington, D.C.)--Juvenile literature. 2. Lincoln, Abraham, 1809-1865--Monuments--Washington (D.C.)--Juvenile literature. 3. Washington (D.C.)--Buildings, structures, etc.--Juvenile literature. I. Title.
  F203.4.L73C37 2014
  975.3--dc23
                                                            2012044671

Printed in the United States of America in North Mankato, Minnesota
1 2 3 4 5 6 7 8 9 0 16 15 14 13 12

122012   Senior Editor: Aaron Carr
WEP301112   Designer: Mandy Christiansen

Every reasonable effort has been made to trace ownership and to obtain permission to reprint copyright material. The publishers would be pleased to have any errors or omissions brought to their attention so that they may be corrected in subsequent printings.

Weigl acknowledges Getty Images as the primary image supplier for this title.

CONTENTS

2 AV² Book Code
4 What is the Lincoln Memorial?
7 A National Symbol
8 Planning the Memorial
11 Building the Memorial
12 Choosing the Stones
15 Carving the Sculpture
16 Writing on the Wall
19 Around the Memorial
21 The Lincoln Memorial Today
22 Lincoln Memorial Facts
24 Key Words/Log on to www.av2books.com

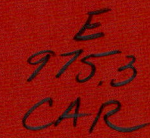

What is the Lincoln Memorial?

The Lincoln Memorial is a large statue of Abraham Lincoln. There is also a building around the statue. The memorial is in Washington, D.C.

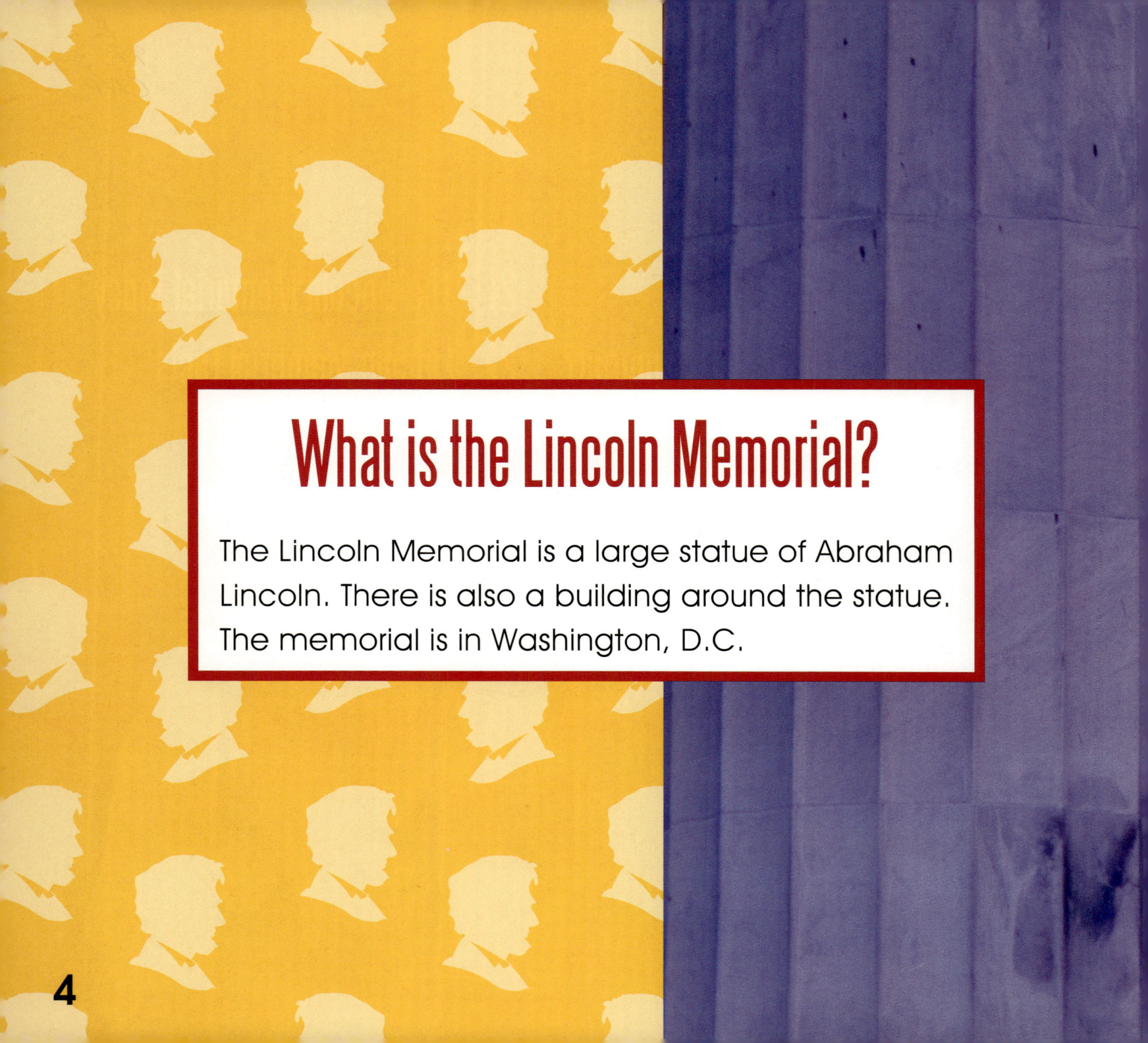

A National Symbol

The Lincoln Memorial was made to honor Abraham Lincoln. He was the 16th president of the United States. He is known for helping all Americans to be free.

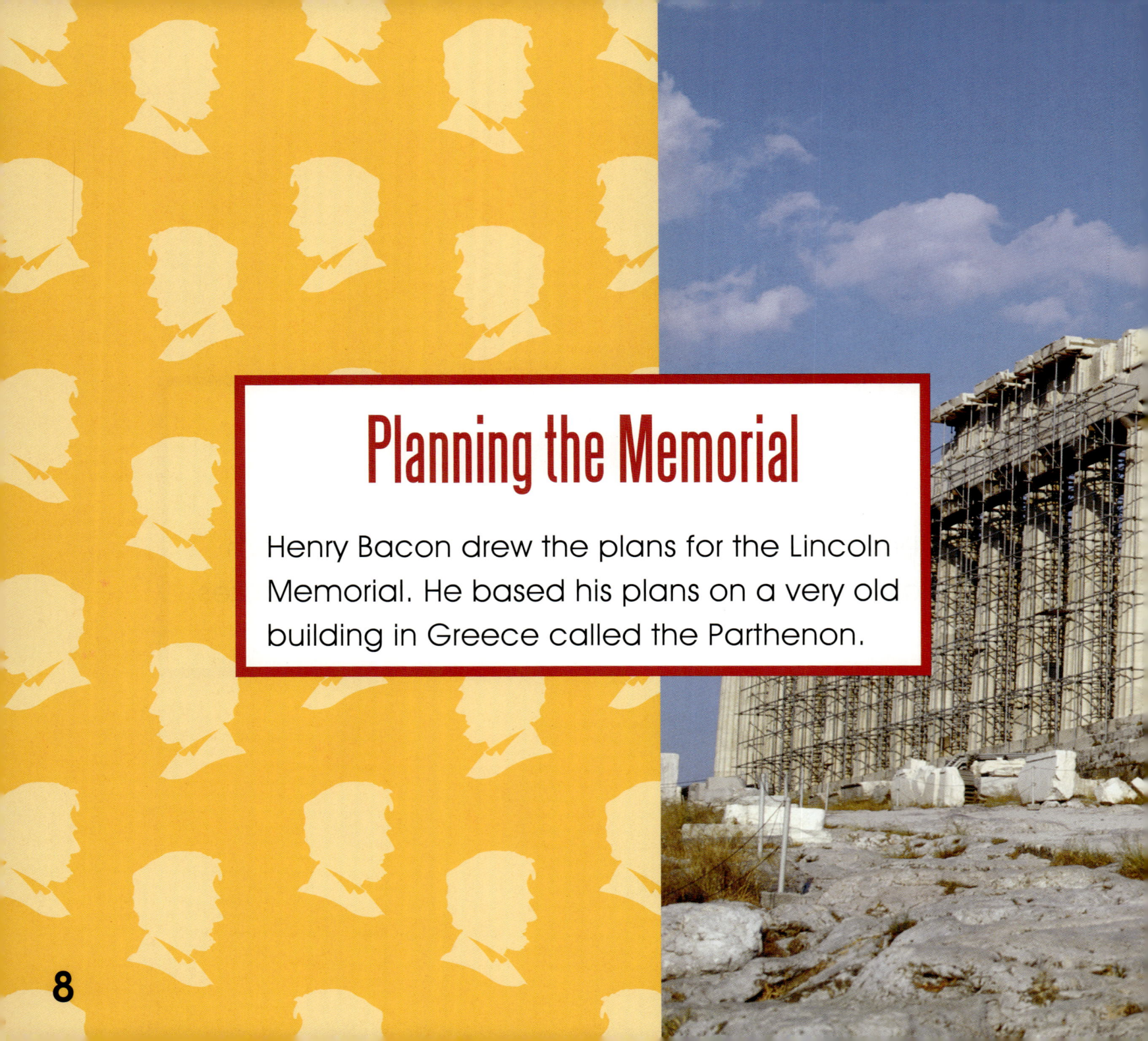

Planning the Memorial

Henry Bacon drew the plans for the Lincoln Memorial. He based his plans on a very old building in Greece called the Parthenon.

9

Building the Memorial

The Lincoln Memorial took eight years to build. Many people worked together to build the memorial.

Choosing the Stones

Three kinds of stones were used to make the memorial. The stones came from six different states. The statue is made from 28 stone blocks.

Carving the Sculpture

Seven people carved the statue of Lincoln. A team of six brothers carved the shape of the statue. Another artist carved the fine details to finish the statue.

Writing on the Wall

Abraham Lincoln gave a famous speech during the Civil War. It is called the Gettysburg Address. The words to this speech are written on the wall of the Lincoln Memorial.

Around the Memorial

There are 36 columns around the memorial. They stand for the 36 states that made up the United States when Lincoln died.

20

The Lincoln Memorial Today

The Lincoln Memorial is one of the most popular places to visit in Washington, D.C. Millions of people visit the memorial each year.

LINCOLN MEMORIAL FACTS

These pages provide detailed information that expands on the interesting facts found in the book. These pages are intended to be used by adults to help young readers round out their knowledge of each national symbol featured in the *American Icons* series.

Pages 4–5  **What is the Lincoln Memorial?** The Lincoln Memorial is one of the best-known monuments in the Washington National Mall. It features a 19-foot (5.8-meter) tall, 175-ton (159-tonne) statue of Abraham Lincoln. The statue is in a building that is 192 feet (59 m) tall, 202 feet (62 m) long, and about 132 feet (40 m) wide.

Pages 6–7  **A National Symbol** Abraham Lincoln is one of the best-known presidents in American history. He was the president during the Civil War, from 1861 to 1865. Lincoln is remembered for his role in keeping the United States together and for ending slavery across the country. He is often called the Great Emancipator.

Pages 8–9  **Planning the Memorial** Plans for the memorial were approved by Congress in 1911. The memorial was designed by New York architect Henry Bacon. He was inspired by the Parthenon, a famous building in Athens, Greece, that is more than 2,000 years old. Bacon later won a gold medal from the American Institute of Architects for his work on the Lincoln Memorial.

Pages 10–11  **Building the Memorial** Workers began construction on the Lincoln Memorial in 1914. Most of the outer building construction was finished by 1917, but the start of World War I caused work on the memorial to slow. The memorial officially opened to the public in 1922.

Pages 12–13  **Choosing the Stones** Henry Bacon chose several types of stones from different parts of the United States. The memorial uses granite from Massachusetts, limestone from Indiana, and marble from Colorado, Tennessee, Alabama, and Georgia. These stones represent the Union Lincoln worked to preserve.

Pages 14–15  **Carving the Sculpture** Daniel Chester French led the team that carved the statue of Lincoln. He studied photos of Lincoln, read historical reports, and examined casts of Lincoln's hands to ensure the statue was accurate. French created a model of the statue. The six Piccirilli brothers then carved marble blocks to match the model. French carved the fine details to finish the statue.

Pages 16–17  **Writing on the Wall** The Battle of Gettysburg was one of the most important battles of the Civil War. The battlefield later became a national cemetery to honor those who died in the fighting. At the opening of the cemetery, Abraham Lincoln gave a famous speech, the Gettysburg Address. The words to this speech are inscribed on one of the walls at the memorial.

Pages 18–19  **Around the Memorial** The Lincoln Memorial was designed to represent the concept of unity through its architectural features. The memorial is surrounded by 36 fluted Doric columns that stand for the 36 states in the Union at the time of Lincoln's death. When the memorial was completed, the names of the 48 states in the Union at that time were carved into outside walls of the memorial.

Pages 20–21  **The Lincoln Memorial Today** People come from around the world to visit the Lincoln Memorial each year. It is one of the best-known tourist attractions of the Washington National Mall. More than 25 million people visit the National Mall and its many monuments, including the Lincoln Memorial, every year.

KEY WORDS

Research has shown that as much as 65 percent of all written material published in English is made up of 300 words. These 300 words cannot be taught using pictures or learned by sounding them out. They must be recognized by sight. This book contains 49 common sight words to help young readers improve their reading fluency and comprehension. This book also teaches young readers several important content words, such as nouns. These words are paired with pictures to aid in learning and improve understanding.

Page	Sight Words First Appearance
4	a, also, around, in, is, large, of, the, there, what
7	all, Americans, be, for, he, made, to, was
8	his, old, on, very
11	many, people, together, took, years
12	came, different, from, kinds, make, states, three, used, were
15	another
16	are, it, this, words
19	that, they, up, when
21	each, most, one, places

Page	Content Words First Appearance
4	Abraham Lincoln, building, Lincoln Memorial, statue, Washington, D.C.
7	free, president, symbol, United States
8	Henry Bacon, Greece, Parthenon, plans
12	blocks, stones
15	artist, brothers, details, sculpture, shape, team
16	Civil War, Gettysburg Address, speech, wall
19	columns

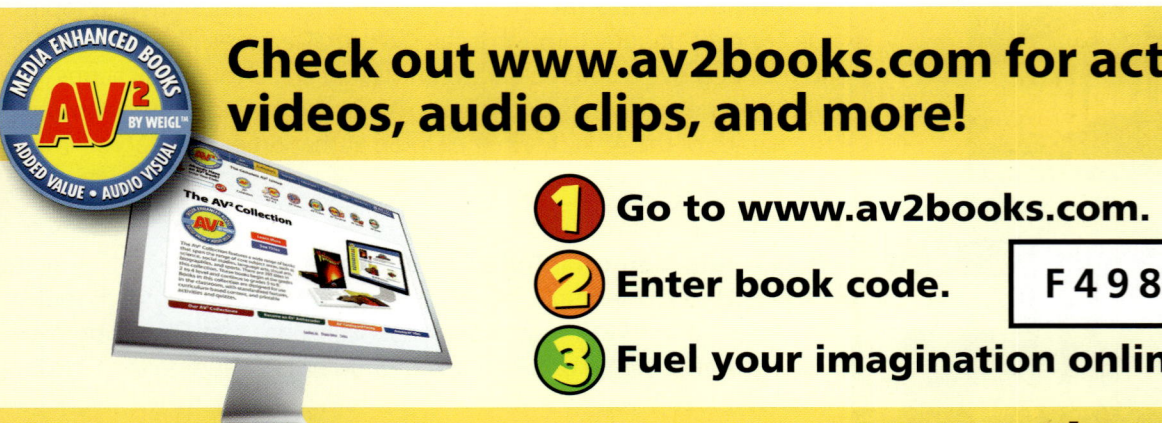

Check out www.av2books.com for activities, videos, audio clips, and more!

1 Go to www.av2books.com.

2 Enter book code. F 4 9 8 3 5 1

3 Fuel your imagination online!

www.av2books.com

4-17-15